391.41 SCA

CHIC
SIMPLE
Components

"A sweet disorder in
the dress kindles in clothes a
wantonness."

ROBERT HERRICK

CHIC
SIMPLE
Components

S C A R V E S

THAMES AND HUDSON

FIRST PUBLISHED IN GREAT BRITAIN IN 1993
BY THAMES AND HUDSON LTD, LONDON

KIM JOHNSON GROSS   JEFF STONE

WRITTEN BY CHRISTA WORTHINGTON
PHOTOGRAPHS BY JOSÉ PICAYO
ICON ILLUSTRATION BY ERIC HANSEN
RESEARCHED BY KIMBERLY PASQUALE
STYLED BY ROBERT RUFINO

DESIGN AND ART DIRECTION BY ROBERT VALENTINE
INCORPORATED

British Library Cataloguing-in-Publication Data
A catalogue record for this book is available from the British Library
ISBN 0-500-01592-9

Printed and bound in Mexico

CONTENTS

THE SCARF

A garment unto itself: the scarf's history, design, and fabric

11

WEARING

From halter to sarong, the art of tying the scarf

35

ACCESSORIES

In the home or the wardrobe, the scarf reinvents itself

65

FIRST AID

Care and cleaning

80

WHERE

Worldwide guide: retail, outlets, and catalogues

85

"The more you know, the less you need."

AUSTRALIAN ABORIGINAL SAYING

T H E   S C A R F

Service and style meet on the formless ground of the
scarf—all texture, color, pattern, and tactility, with no
set shape. It simplifies through reinvention. The scarf is
the ultimate Chic Simple item, capable of clothing both
the home and the body, as an accent or a main event.

"A scarf is the most versatile accessory. It
can be worn as a belt, a necklace, to tie back
hair on a bad hair day—even as a skirt."

DONNA KARAN

THE HISTORY OF THE SCARF.

SINCE THE LOINCLOTH, THE SCARF HAS FUNCTIONED AS A GARMENT unto itself, worn by the ancients with dazzling simplicity. Only in this century has the Western woman fully seized the scarf's genius. As corsets and Victorian morals fell away, the

EMPRESS JOSEPHINE

Empress Josephine owned three hundred cashmere shawls, worth the contemporary equivalent of millions; her husband, Napoleon, would occasionally throw them into the fire, annoyed by how much of her body they concealed.

"Adieu, my friends

Isadora Duncan's last words before her scarf caught in the wheel of the Bugatti in

scarf became a flag of movement. It accompanied women into convertibles and into the office, where it was a badge of common purpose in wartime. By now, the scarf has acquired as many faces as femininity. Like blue jeans, it is worn by each person in a different way.

MARILYN MONROE

Marilyn Monroe posed in her last photo shoot holding a chiffon square between her bare breasts and the camera. That image was silkscreened onto a scarf by photographer Bert Stern in 1967.

SEX AND THE SCARF

*Redolent with scent, the scarf has been a romantic talisman
since the medieval knight took his lady's hanky into battle. In myth,
the scarf—especially the veil—is the symbolic skin of the soul. A tool of
temptation and seduction as when Salome danced for the head of John
the Baptist, it can also evoke sexual inhibition, modesty, and the devotion
of nuns. Matadors' capes and magicians' chiffons defy death and
incredulity. Throughout literature, lovers' kerchiefs have linked mind
and heart, scent and sensibility, often with dire consequences.
Othello would not have killed Desdemona but for what he believed was
a trail of deception left by her hanky.*

'm bound for glory."

was riding and broke her neck.

SHAWL MANIA

*The folds of antiquity as draped in the shawl enthralled eighteenth-
and nineteenth-century Europeans and painters (Jacques-Louis David).
Lady Emma Hamilton inspired Goethe to rhapsody with her shawl dances,
performed for friends and imitated by the celebrated French hostess
Madame Récamier; Elisabeth Vigée-Lebrun posed and draped shawls over
friends in painterly "tableaux vivants." The presence of this handwoven
bit of cloth proved that one was rich enough to afford the high price of
something imported from Kashmir.*

Shapes. Scarves can be reduced to the geometry of the oblong and the square—the shapes of the looms that first wove them. But each swings from a different emotional axis: the oblong has been associated with ethereal, intellectual, and romantic tendencies since the ecclesiastical stole. Hindu yogis maintain that a scarf at the neck helps free the fifth chakra of communication—accounting, perhaps, for the way aesthetes and poets have clung to it. The square is historically more earthbound, an emblem of home, hearth, and contained femininity. The Romantics believed that the square shawl stoked emotion by framing the heart.

THE LARGE
SQUARE
(48" plus)
shawl, pareo,
sarong, halter

THE POCKET
SQUARE
(16 x 18") pocket
square or
handkerchief

14

THE OBLONG

(14 x 54") cravat,
muffler, jabot,
sash, stole, turban

**THE CLASSIC
SQUARE**

(36")
kerchief or
neckerchief

Fabric. The primal pleasure of a scarf comes from the fabric of which it is made. Its "hand" (feel), texture, color, and way of reflecting light all combine to create a sensory language, a code based on the fabric's fiber. A scarf is imbued with a woman's fragrance like an intimate calling card. Ancient Ionians invented pleats to enhance the way it draped, a technique later copied by Fortuny. Prehistoric weavers tufted wool to mimic fur. From the start, fabric has been a second skin that subliminally describes character. The use of contrasting fabrics—an iridescent scarf against dull black—heightens the effect of both.

In the nineteenth century, the British could not sell their homemade versions of Indian shawls without dousing them in patchouli—the Bengali lavender with which the imported originals were perfumed.

SILK SECRETS
It is said that silk was discovered when a cocoon from the larva of a Bombyx mori moth fell from a mulberry tree into the teacup of the Chinese Empress Hsi Ling-shi in the third millennium B.C., and she opened it and found a glistening thread.

(12 x 76" oblong) Th
reversible scarf heighte
the experience of fabr
through contrast of
texture, color, and
pattern.

Reversible. Well-made topcoats and black-tie play host to the reversible muffler—the masculine classic long appropriated by women for its sensuality and versatility. It suggests discretion and a soft, private underside that won't be revealed to just anyone. Like the bicolored stoles of the clergy, from which it may have been derived, the reversible muffler celebrates fabric in a way that indulges the senses but is somehow sober—the definition of high style. All scarves benefit by being faced in unmatched fabric. The extra cost pays off in service and value—one garment leading a double life.

Pattern. Rhyme and a refreshing lack of reason have been pattern's gifts to mankind. Pattern is an emotional Morse code. It can be woven into a scarf (as with plaids and ikats), printed onto the surface in symmetrical repetition called "repeats," or spread in painterly free-form. Silkscreens—stencils through which dye is squeezed one color at a time—produce the precision color of luxury silk head scarves.

"The repetitions of patterns give us rest. The marvels of designs stir the imagination."

OSCAR WILDE

CLOCKWISE FROM
TOP LEFT

Golden bridles, bits, and horsey paraphernalia on the status-laden Hermès scarf perversely play well with working man's jeans.

For centuries, geometrics have made order out of chaos, and polka dots have made us smile.

Tribal tartan, the flag of warring Scottish clansmen, has come to represent rural harmony.

Nineteenth-century Europeans sought out fabrics that were exotic and rare. Hence the craze for paisley, here printed on velvet.

"A scarf becomes something different
upon each different wearer. I see scarves
. . . as tools for the wearer's creativity."

ISSEY MIYAKE

Detail. The way a scarf is edged helps define its character. A clean edge is neat, and if hand rolled, luxurious. At Hermès, a staff of sixty seamstresses called *roulotteuses* (rollers) specialize in tacking rolled edges down with neat stitches. Fringe celebrates movement and can be sporty on a wool muffler or festive in silk, changing mood with material: a border of pearls, raffia, New Age crystals, or antique beads each strikes its own attitude. Self-fringe, an edge of unwoven threads that looks as if the loom stopped weaving, is casual in wool, dressier in silk taffeta. Pattern, too, can function like a frame, setting "repeat" prints in a border of color.

WHY FRINGE?

Fringe was invented by the caveman in imitation of animal hair, in fur and cut leather. A Bronze Age scarf buried in a peat bog in Ireland was found fringed with tufts of horsehair. Tassels are also prehistoric and mimic the fur tails of animals.

STITCHING

Fagoting, a stitched, open seam, often used in linen, is an elegant legacy of Madeleine Vionnet, who used it to pioneer seemingly seamless shape in fashion. The rolled silk scarf is stitched either entirely by hand or by machine with corners handstitched.

"For me a scarf is like a postcard, a souvenir, or a memento."

GIANNI VERSACE

THE ART SCARF

Henri Matisse, Paul Cézanne, and Raoul Dufy were among the first in a crowd of artists whose work was the inspiration for a scarf. The scarf at left, by British fabric designers Timney & Fowler, is an homage to Calder.

THE TRAVEL SCARF

On the wave of tourism that struck America and Europe after World War II, the souvenir scarf became a sartorial postcard and a collector's item.

The Simple Scarf. The bandanna. Cowboys called it a "wipe." The work ethic of this cotton square is mythic. It soaked up sweat and screened out dust all along the American frontier as dutifully as denim, which it has always adorned. For its utility, it has become the blue jeans of scarves: a unisex basic worn the world over. Probably named after the Hindu word for tie-dye (*bandhnu*), the colorful printed bandanna was adapted from the Spanish ranchero's scarf worn in Mexico. Cowboy neckerchiefs were earth-colored at first, as camouflage on the range. Today, this scarf is the banner of railwaymen and ranchers, Roy Rogers and the Reagans, the Grunge and Gap cultures, old-timers and tots—even dogs. Its wholesome appeal is not without a whiff of adventure: the pirate's kerchief and the bandit's mask are its ancestors. For all its contribution to style, it remains a humble "wipe"—it's still the handkerchief carried by those who have yet to succumb to Kleenex, or plan to rob a train.

5

SCARVES

SQUARE
MUFFLER
SHAWL
STOLE
PAREO

Basics. Shopping for scarves is like strategizing a wardrobe—look for fundamentals on which to build. Pattern and color are the decorative wild cards that pull one in on impulse. But shape is a clearer indicator of how a scarf will work. Consider seasonal criteria of warmth and weight. The temperate seasons of spring and fall put shawls and large squares of silk and wool challis into service. Summer is the time of the cotton pareo, the body wrap of Polynesia. The stole is inherently elegant, an evening natural. The muffler is functional or festive depending on fabric—a woolen workhorse in winter.

Basics. First, remember that scarves are just clothes. Like the basic tops, pants, and jackets that hang in your closet and provide the framework of daily dress, basic scarves are versatile and adaptable to every occasion. They are colored to blend with the other elements of your wardrobe, shaped to move the way you do, and scaled to comfort and proportion. Push classics to their natural limits and the scarf that qualifies as an authentic basic will emerge, like Venus on the half-shell, from the sea of poseurs. Think literally. The cashmere muffler comes in no more appropriate shade than pearl gray. The silk square is most feminine in floral. The evening shawl really shines when it's iridescent. The summer pareo is as light on the skin as a warm breeze and exotic when it's patterned in an authentic South Sea batik. A rural plaid shawl should be able to wrap the heroines of *Tess of the D'Urbervilles, Wuthering Heights,* or you. Scarves should not be viewed merely as an accessory to your wardrobe but as a wardrobe in itself.

CASHMERE MUFFLER

(17 x 55" oblong)
In winter, the essential scarf

PLAID WOOL SHAWL

(56" square) For day or night—romantic and functional

COTTON PAREO

(40 x 87" oblong) Summer's travel companion, for beach, evening, or day

SILK OR METALLIC STOLE

(30 x 95" oblong) An evening stole in a sensual fabric works as jewelry for evening.

W E A R I N G

A sense of helplessness tends to overcome the average woman when faced with tying a scarf. If it's well tied, the scarf relaxes the look of what it's worn with. The key is not to fight the fluidity of fabric but to let it flow.

"Sometimes I see people wearing scarves in a strange manner. You can tell somebody's told them how to tie it. . . . They torture the poor scarves into looking like necklaces. It's dreadful. The beauty of a scarf is that it flows, that it has movement."

PALOMA PICASSO

The Head. The head scarf reveals as it conceals. Since the fifteenth century—when the Catholic Church decreed that the Virgin Mary conceived through her ear—wrapping the head has been a show of feminine chastity with built-in provocations. The louder the "go away" message, the more audible the "come hither." That sexual hide-and-seek is relieved by sturdy purpose: shelter from the elements. The touring scarf, knotted at the back of the neck, was born with the automobile and came of age riding in the Fifties' convertible. It's a more elegant, racy version of the Queen Elizabeth at Balmoral-in-the-rain look—which knots once under the chin.

THE TOURING SCARF

(36" square)
With a square, cross under the chin and tie at the nape of the neck. With an oblong, wrap around the neck without knotting.

HIDING BEHIND THE SCARF

Marilyn Monroe wore one when she went in front of the news cameras in Beverly Hills to announce her divorce from Joe DiMaggio.

Covering the chin has been considered feminine since 1200 B.C., when the Assyrians first ruled that women must veil their faces in public.

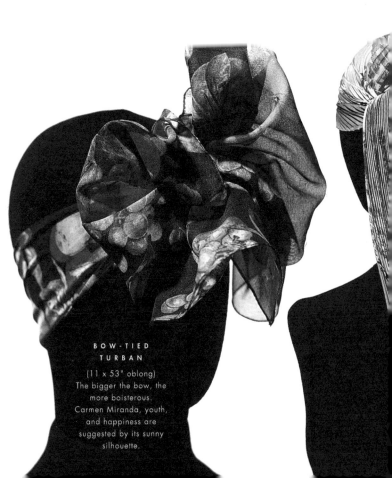

**BOW-TIED
TURBAN**

(11 x 53" oblong)
The bigger the bow, the
more boisterous.
Carmen Miranda, youth,
and happiness are
suggested by its sunny
silhouette.

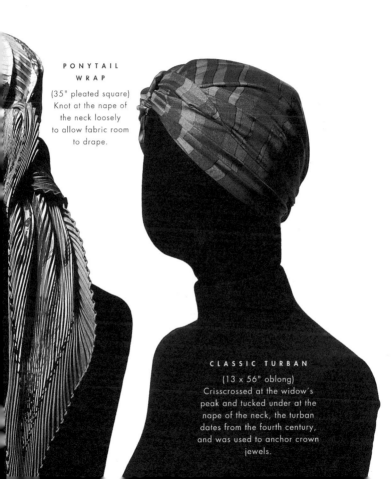

PONYTAIL WRAP

(35" pleated square)
Knot at the nape of
the neck loosely
to allow fabric room
to drape.

CLASSIC TURBAN

(13 x 56" oblong)
Crisscrossed at the widow's
peak and tucked under at the
nape of the neck, the turban
dates from the fourth century,
and was used to anchor crown
jewels.

(56" square)
The simplest way to
wear a scarf: crossed
under the chin and
tossed over each
shoulder

Head Wrap. The simplest head wrap is also the most feminine. Evocative of rural landscapes and romantic heroines from Lara to the French Lieutenant's Woman, the untied head scarf, crossed under the chin and draped over the back of each shoulder, is secured only by its own weight. It appeals through vulnerability. Sheer fabric makes it more sophisticated. Though just one step removed from the movie-star look of knotting the head wrap at the nape of the neck, it is sartorial miles from it in mood. It lacks all severity and hauteur. It is simple and serviceable as well as romantic. In winter, it is a sensible alternative to a hat, and suited to the textures of wool and knit.

"Scarves can be humorous, enchanting, amusing and alluring. Almost like gloves, they express degrees of humanity."

GEOFFREY BEENE

EXOTIC WEAVE

(10 1/2 x 34" oblong)
With eight-inch fringe,
textural intrigue for
evening, iridescent and
translucent

BANDANNA TIE

(36" square)
Like the ascot, but tied
in the manner of the
bandit scarf, wrapped
around the back of the
neck and knotted in front

BULKY MUFFLER

(13 x 68" oblong)
Wrapped twice around
the neck and knotted in
front with a nubby
handcrafted texture
and a self-fringe

Neck and Shoulders. Getting the scarf to take shape is a matter of folding it down to your size. The more prominent one's facial features and bone structure, the more dramatic the sweep one can carry. Whatever one's physiognomy, tying a scarf still requires some finesse. Aim for a strategic balance of energy and insouciance. As designer Geoffrey Beene puts it: "A scarf should never just hang. It should look as if it has performed, and should not look extraneous to what it's worn with." As a frame for the face, it's most flattering when slightly askew. Avoid the Boy Scout silhouette in which the knot dangles over the heart; it can look dowdy.

DOUBLED-UP MUFFLER

(13 x 51" oblong)
Tied through its own loop, the cashmere muffler (far left) secures itself and shrinks to a flattering frame for the face.

SHAWL

(56" square)
Knotted at the shoulder, this lightweight wool challis provides a more casual frame.

THE LYING SCARF

The French called the scarf that enhanced the dimensions of the bustline the fichu menteur—*the lying scarf—worn in the eighteenth century to fill in the bare necklines of open coats and dresses.*

Global

Usage. Whether it's used for carrying babies or berries, displaying crown jewels, or doing a belly dance, the scarf is a sartorial tool which every continent has made its own. Religion, politics, and ideas traveled from east to west with the scarf along the Silk Road. Its global reach shrank, however, and the body drape was considered primitive until dancer and choreographer Isadora Duncan and couturier Paul Poiret revived the logic of clothes that swing from the axis of the shoulders rather than from the waist. Ever since, the West has been discovering what Polynesians have known all along: a scarf can simplify life.

WISDOM OF THE WEAVE

The language encoded in fabric is as prized as scripture in India.
Weavers are valued, in the manner of mandarins or monks,
as keepers of cherished tradition and were usually exchanged as parts
of dowries or as prizes of political conquest.

Cleopatra was one of the first Westerners in recorded history
to wear silk. Until the sixth century B.C., the penalty for smuggling
silkworms out of China was death.

In nineteenth-century France, a woman's native village could be
deduced from the way she wore her kerchief.

VARIATIONS ON THE SCARF

The Indian sari is considered the world's most feminine form of dress.
A garment unto itself, it's sold in different sizes of oblong, and distinguished
by plain or fancy fabrics. The outer end-piece of the sari is woven for extra
strength to serve as a sack around the waist, back, or hip and to keep
the sun off anything carried on the head.

The Indian dhoti is the male version of the sari—a long skirt with one
end wrapped through the legs and tucked up into the waistband.

The loincloth: adopted by Egyptians in 3000 B.C.
and still worn.

Tops. The halter top—technically, one that ties around the neck to leave the back exposed—has been worn and bought by women as a cut-and-sewn garment when it is actually a form of scarf. As a style, it underwent booming popularity in the Thirties—glamorous with its seductive simplicity. The halter offers style and comfort: It is made to relieve the heat of both nightclubs and summer. For evening, it solves the problem of what to wear beneath a jacket when only a bit of color and minimum cover are required. The bustier wrap eliminates the neckline altogether, and looks best on the broad-shouldered.

BUSTIER

(26$\frac{1}{2}$ x 67" oblong)
When knotted over the breastbone, it replaces a strapless top. This striped version "shapes" the torso.

DOUBLE HALTER

(two 24" squares)
Crisscrossed pattern, tied at the back of the neck and the waist

HALSTON

In the Seventies, American designer Halston made the halter top contiguous with the dress, in slinky silk jersey—not unlike scarf fabric. Halston shared a love of pure line with dancer and choreographer Martha Graham, who sometimes danced with scarves, and he designed costumes for her dance company.

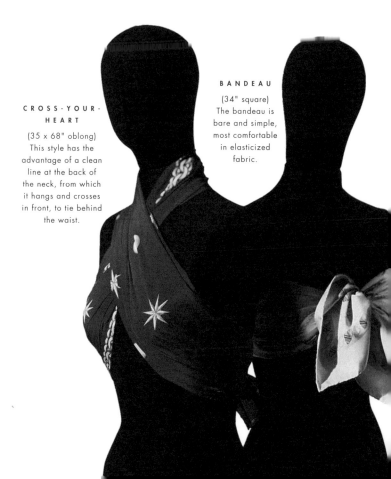

CROSS-YOUR-HEART

(35 x 68" oblong)
This style has the advantage of a clean line at the back of the neck, from which it hangs and crosses in front, to tie behind the waist.

BANDEAU

(34" square)
The bandeau is bare and simple, most comfortable in elasticized fabric.

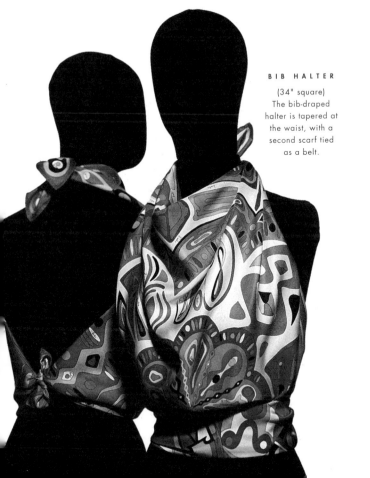

BIB HALTER

(34" square)
The bib-draped
halter is tapered at
the waist, with a
second scarf tied
as a belt.

SARONG SKIRT

(28 x 63" oblong)
Wrapped at the waist,
with a print border
drawing a line across
the hip

SARONG DRES

(43 x 69" oblong)
Wrapped in front, tie
at the chest, and belte
with a scarf

Sarong. Hollywood can take some of the credit for getting Westerners to wear South Sea sarongs. Sarongs, traditionally five to seven yards of cloth wrapped around the torso and tied at the waist or chest, can serve as the versatile mainstay of an entire holiday wardrobe. The typical Polynesian pareo (pronounced "parayo"), identical in shape and form to a sarong, is patterned with floral batik—an East Indian method of wax printing cotton that was popular on "peasant" fabric in the Sixties. This sultry way of dressing can be seen today at suburban poolsides or on city streets, but it will always make one think of toes in the sand and palm trees.

ROAD TO SARONG
OR
THE PAREO
PRINCESS

From the moment Dorothy Lamour kept house for Bob Hope and Bing Crosby on a South Sea island in the 1940 film Road to Singapore, *dressed only in a skimpy sarong, there was no turning back. When the movie heroine of the tropics modeled tailored versions of the Tahitian and Balinese originals, it was clear that the sarong had traveled west. "Pareo" and "sarong" refer to both the fabric and the fashion, worn by men and women of the Pacific islands.*

BLANKET SKIRT

(Blanket size: 60 x 60")
Wrapped at the waist
with a leather belt, the
blanket skirt is one of the
earliest forms of dress.
From 2700 B.C., the
Sumerians wore fringed
cloth of crudely woven
wool wrapped around
the body.

SILK
SEERSUCKER
WRAP

(28 x 63" oblong)
Stretchy texture holds
shape with a knot in
front.

BATIK DRESS

(43 x 69" oblong)
Tied at the back of the
neck, halter style, the
batik dress wraps closed
over the buttocks, belted
by a batik scarf.

Pants. Scarves have been draped and tied in the form of pants since antiquity. What Asian Indians call a dhoti, and Cambodians a sampot, is a graceful response to hot climates—fabric wrapped around the waist like a sarong, with one end brought forward between the legs and tucked into the waistband. Fluidity and practicality merge in a single garment. This variation wraps vertically, down the body and up through the legs, rather than across the hips, with the advantage of leaving the thigh exposed—either bare or under leggings. The languor of the look is enhanced by lightweight, gauzy fabric, especially if it's translucent.

HAREM PANTS
(75 x 36")
Tie one end of the oblong around the waist, and knot it in back with the fabric unfurled before you. Pull the far end of the fabric between the knees, and up over the buttocks to the waist, where it wraps over the hips to tie in front.

SARI FACTS
The Indian sari is also called the lugda, dhoti or pata, depending on where and how it's worn. Although it is a single piece of fabric, each area of the oblong has a different name according to its position and function on the body when it is wrapped. In some parts of India, the end fringe is cut and offered to the community goddess before the sari is worn.

EVENING SHAWL

(67 x 35" oblong)
Reversible silk jacquard
shawl, tapered into
long tassels

Evening. As a diadem for the body, the evening shawl or scarf has a dual agenda. It dazzles through fabric—cut velvet, metallic, lace, chiffon, silk—color, and sheen but soothes with simplicity of form. The fact that something so jewel-like and luxurious on the surface could be carefree makes it compelling. Victorian women knew the inherent provocations of the shawl—the way its surface could elicit excitement through color and texture without diminishing its sense of propriety. From that appreciation, the contemporary scarf has followed. It can deliver a jolt of color that might overwhelm a fitted garment. It can catch light and manifest mood in its folds. For evening, the wrap can stage a spectacle without sacrificing elegance and simplicity.

DOT SPEAK *There's something inexplicably humorous and playful about polka dots—and the larger the dot, the greater the effect. Small polka dots, however, can be sophisticated and even demure; when big dots are combined with stripes, they become ritualized, even theatrical.*

SCARF JACKET

(25 x 83" oblong)
Reversible evening
wrap with sleeves, cut
low to waist to accent
drape and emphasize
sweep, double-faced
in silk brocade

"I love silk neck scarves for evening, it's like a jet cloud in tulle."

GEOFFREY BEENE

Tulle. The ultimate fashion illusion, tulle is barely there. It can be seen through, but it's not fragile—it's often made of nylon. It holds all the sexual dynamite of the veil, signaling the control of chastity (on the virgin bride) and its imminent release. It can be seriously elegant or when ruffled or frilly, simply festive. In black, tulle can settle seamlessly over any category of clothing, from velvet pants to ball gowns. Traditionally of gauze or silk, this hexagonal-net fabric is a foil for decoration—beads, pearls, and "airborne" appliqués. It holds a lofty shape without a struggle or drapes dramatically into a transparent train.

TRAIN OF TULLE

(51 x 165")
Black ruffled tulle scarf with appliqués. Bearer of glad tidings—tulle is festive with confetti-like pieces of fabric attached on both sides.

HOW-TO

The easiest way to appliqué tulle is to glue bits of felt to it, but do so on both sides of the fabric. A more finished job would include stitching the edges of any appliqués.

THE VEIL

Women have worn veils for 2,500 years. The Bible called for the wearing of veils as a prophylactic against male lust. In the Middle Ages only virgins went about with uncovered heads.

ACCESSORIES

Scarves contain, wrap, and cover in ways that are limited only by one's imagination. They carry color, pattern, and even humor in a form that can turn a simple square or rectangle into art or object, into something to wear or perhaps to sit on. Needle and thread, or in some cases, scissors, glue, or staples, can be applied to the scarf to reinvent it as something else.

"The scarf is the perfect nomadic accessory. You can use it on furniture or on yourself. It can be an improvised tablecloth in a hotel room. Scarves can become anything. You need an extra bag? They become a bag."

DIANE VON FURSTENBERG

THE POUCH BAG

Scarves fold naturally into a pouch, stitched or tied to make an ad hoc satchel

Handbag. The scarf made its first appearance in history as a satchel, and it still lends itself to that purpose naturally. Tied as a pouch, it can carry lipstick and keys for an evening, pack jewelry on a trip, or wrap a gift. The scarf's association with the bag became more a function of status seeking in the Sixties, when the patterned silk squares of Hermès and Pucci were first tied to the handles of Kelly handbags like flags of the cognoscenti.

EMILIO PUCCI *Transforming scarves into other garments was the talent of Emilio Pucci, who made swirling psychedelic color and geometric pattern the craze of the Sixties, and now classic. His fashion career was launched when he made a dress from several scarves stitched together. With the scarf as his icon of fluid, interchangeable clothing, he pioneered the ready-to-wear uniform: comfortable silk jersey dresses and Lycra jumpsuits that traveled from day to evening and accommodated all circumstances with warm color and cheer. Helen Gurley Brown, the editor of* Cosmopolitan *magazine, declared that her Puccis made her so happy she would like to be buried in them. Currently, a thirty-six-inch silk Pucci scarf sells for about $200. (In 1965, they retailed for $20.)*

Options. Scarves fill in when other accessories fade or collapse—a watchband worn to the breaking point, or shoes that need refinishing. But they can also be a personalizing option—the pattern you use to make an object your own. A utilitarian item—an eyeglass case, for instance—gains gaiety and charm under the influence of color and print. Experiment with contrast by tying odd bandannas together to make a belt. Make sure to match fabric to function. Heavier silks are naturally resistant to rain and scuffing and were the traditional fabric of umbrellas, until they became mass-produced items to be thrown away.

WATCH
(12" square)
Turn a kerchief or bandanna into a patterned watchband.

SHOES
Shoes can be recovered in scarves made of silk faille or velvet—but just once. Approximate price per refurbished pair: $150.

EYEGLASS CASE
(12" square)
Take a scarf and make a drawstring tote with padded backing for your glasses.

UMBRELLA
(46" square)
To cover an umbrella requires a scarf in a weave dense enough to resist rain when treated with water repellent. A recovering job costs about $85.

one

H U N D R E D   S C A R V E S

What you do with a scarf is your own business, but consider this: At their best, scarves marry ornament and utility. Kerchief-covered lampshades, with tails dangling, evoked the mood of the Casbah so savored in the 1960s, but they also softened the light before dimmers became a household convenience. That double duty is the scarf's home equity. Think of it as just a piece of cloth and its usefulness will multiply.

GOOD USES

tablecloth LAMPSHADE *shower curtain* UMBRELLA COVER *arm sling*
SUNSHADE *napkin* CUSHION COVER *wall art* WRISTWATCH BAND *headband*
HANKY *belt* SOFA THROW *satchel* BABY CARRIER *garden vegetable tote*
FAREWELL SIGNAL *dust mask* GIFT WRAPPING *rain hat* HAIR SHIELD *skirt*
BEACH BLANKET *dog collar* CURTAIN *shoe cover* HOTEL ROOM SLIPCOVER
cravat SHOE BOX COVER *romantic keepsake pillow* BIKINI *sash* SHAWL
book cover HALTER TOP *fanny pack*

QUESTIONABLE USES

POTHOLDER *bookmark* MEMO PAD *sandwich bag* ICE BUCKET
kite BLINDFOLD *bondage* COFFEE FILTER *hang glider* MAKEUP REMOVER
diaper BIB *tent* SAIL *bandage* LEASH *parachute* HAMMOCK

"If you don't feel great you can put some
bright color around your face with a scarf. It
can be inexpensive cotton. It's not the price
that makes you happy, it's an attitude."

MOTOE, *designer of WovenWind Scarves*

Lampshade. Light has been used to illuminate pattern since Islamic artists designed the peek-a-boo screen. The most artful patterns can be applied to a lampshade without much artistry at all—it just takes vision and a willingness to cut and paste scarves to transform a generic shade into something unique. Match or contrast the color and mood of the scarf design to the material of the lamp. Vertical lines on a pattern can acquire mesmeric momentum when spiraled around the cone of a shade. But resist the temptation to throw fabric over a lampshade without regard for safety concerns: Be sure to first apply flame retardant to fabric, which is available at retail outlets.

HOW-TO

1. Make a paper pattern of the shade by taping tissue paper around it and trimming the paper top and bottom with a razor to fit the dimensions. The yoke-shaped pattern that results can be placed flat onto a scarf. 2. Tape the edges of the pattern to the scarf to keep it in place, then cut the scarf to the pattern, and remove the paper. 3. Apply spray-on glue to the surface of the lampshade and mold the scarf onto it. 4. Smooth out wrinkles by touching a warm iron to the shade. 5. Glue prefolded binding around the top and bottom edges to finish.

Chair. As in fashion, a sense of style comes into the home through a mix of elements that involves the play of genre, color, and mood on a single piece of furniture or throughout an entire room. Pile up pillows on a sofa to experiment. Use odd scarves as seat covers to break up the uniformity of a traditional set of dining chairs. Look for harmony in contrast by covering a couch in a single unifying print but with each cushion in a slightly different hue, or pattern. Any scarf fabric—cotton, silk, or cashmere silk—will work on cushions. Or put a contemporary clock print across the seat of an antique chair to contrast style across time.

H O W - T O

Covering furniture with scarves requires a staple gun, and for the adventurous, a sewing machine. The seat cushions of dining chairs that are mounted on slats of wood are the easiest to work with: lift them out and staple scarves to the cushions' undersides. Large loose slip covers can be stitched, the way clothing and scarf designer Gene Meyer does them, from 44" silk and wool challis scarves. He has also been known to hang four contrasting shades of the same pareo on a single window.

Frame. Some scarf designs look their best when pressed flat and framed. Artists from Matisse to Warhol have deemed silk a worthy canvas; dye on silk can have the artistry of paint on canvas, and often with richer, more sensuous color. The more colors used in a single design, the greater the technical virtuosity of the silkscreen, since each shade has to be applied separately. Hermès boasts that it has the time, the craftsmanship, and the talent to apply as many as forty colors to a single scarf.

HERMÈS *Although it is not the original status scarf, it is certainly the most tenacious. The equestrian-motif Hermès kerchief has been more widely copied than any other item made by this distinguished French saddlery firm, apart perhaps from its Kelly handbag. But the finish that gives the scarves their luxurious sheen remains an inimitable secret. First produced in the nineteenth century with woodblocks, then silkscreened with symmetrical equestrian imagery, Hermès scarves were favored by well-born French women and jet-setters in the 1950s and 1960s for their association with moneyed country life. In the 1970s, Queen Elizabeth permitted a photograph of herself wearing an Hermès scarf to be used on Britain's 17-pence postage stamp. Younger women didn't cling to them en masse until the 1980s, when hysteria set in. Sale day at the Paris headquarters remains a free-for-all that is not fully accounted for by the quality of Hermès craftsmanship.*

Gift wrap. The Japanese are ardent gift givers whose aesthetic is driven by simplicity, and have long practiced the art of gift wrapping with cloth, called *furoshiki*. They manipulate squares of fabric in particular ways to tie up different objects—bottles, flowers, fruit, or boxes—with a gentle symmetry. The care that goes into the presentation is inseparable from that which has gone into the gift. Wrapping with a scarf is thoughtfulness made manifest, increasing the pleasure of the recipient and guaranteeing that nothing gets thrown away.

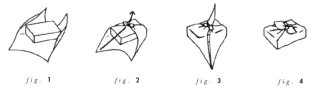

fig. **1** *fig.* **2** *fig.* **3** *fig.* **4**

WRAP RAP

1. Center a rectangular box on a square scarf so that the corners of the scarf meet at its middle and can be tied. **2.** Knot two opposite corners of the scarf together. **3.** Pull the remaining two corners to the center of the box and slip them underneath the first knot. **4.** Tie the ends over the first knot by making a single knot.

first aid.

Scarves are exempt from the Federal Trade Commission law that requires textile clothing and certain piece goods to come with care instructions attached. Some manufacturers attach care labels to scarves, but more often one must make an educated guess as to how to clean them. The more elaborate the weave, the more cautious one must be with cleaning.

DECIPHERING CARE LABELS

A manufacturer or importer is only required to list one method of safe care, even if other safe methods exist. If a garment has a care label with washing instructions, it may or may not be dry-cleanable. There is no way to tell from the label. Some labels do inform consumers of all satisfactory care methods, but they do so on the volition of the manufacturer. If a garment is marked "Dry Clean," as opposed to "Dry Clean Only," and the fabric is constructed simply, you may have the option of laundering it, after you have tested for colorfastness.

WASHING WOOLS

Chlorine bleach will damage wool fibers. Wash in Woolite. Roll in a towel to dry, then block and dry on a flat surface away from direct heat or sunlight. Steaming woolens can refresh them.

CLEANING CASHMERE

Woven cashmere should be dry-cleaned, even if it is not tagged "Dry Clean Only." It may shrink if washed and dyes may run and become blotchy. If it is tagged to indicate that it can also be handwashed, block it flat to dry so it doesn't lose its form. Knit cashmere can be handwashed unless otherwise indicated.

CLEANING SILK

*Generally, silk scarves should be dry-cleaned.
If washed, the consistency of a silk scarf may
be altered depending on the finishing
treatment used to give it sheen. Colors may
run. Chlorine bleach damages silk and
causes it to yellow.*

WASHABLE SILK

*Pre-wash treatments have made more silks
washable. Silks that are often safe to wash
include raw silk, China silk, India silk, crepe
de chine, pongee, shantung, tussah,
douppioni, and jacquard. Roll-dry in a towel
to absorb moisture, then hang on a padded
hanger. Machine drying silk will cause it to
disintegrate. Instead, iron it on a low setting
while slightly damp.*

RISKS OF COLOR-BLEEDING

*If the manufacturer has been negligent, the
dyes on silk and rayon are not always
colorfast to the procedures listed in the care
instructions. Articles labeled as dry-cleanable
will sometimes contain dyes that bleed
extensively when dry-cleaned. Deep colors may
transfer onto lighter areas. Garments labeled
as washable may also bleed and lose color,
especially those in darker colors. If an article
is multicolored, test it for colorfastness before
washing.*

HOW TO TEST FOR COLORFASTNESS

*Find an inconspicuous area on the scarf, wet
the fabric, and blot it with a white cloth.
Allow it to air dry to determine if the dye and
sizing are disturbed.*

CARE OF ACETATE

*100% acetate requires dry-cleaning. Some
blends are handwashable with cool water and
Woolite. Avoid soaking, as acetate is not very
colorfast. Drip dry, and press while still damp
with a cool iron. Do not use steam.*

CARE OF ACRYLIC

*Wrinkle-free and fast-drying, acrylics can be
washed by hand or on a gentle machine cycle
in cool or warm water and Woolite. If
machine drying is recommended, use a low
setting. Iron with moderate heat if necessary.*

CARE OF NYLON

*Wash separately, or in like colors with
Woolite, by hand or on a gentle machine cycle.
Do not dry white nylon in the sun, as
yellowing could occur.*

CARE OF RAYON

*Also known as viscose, rayon is fragile.
Whether it is washable depends upon the
finish, construction, and blend with other
fibers. Do not use chlorine bleach. Rayon can
be stained by water spots.*

CARE OF VELVET

Never iron nylon velvets. Hang velvet on padded hangers; don't fold it. Dry-clean rayon velvet and acetate/rayon velvets. Frequent steaming and brushing with a soft brush can keep velvet fresh between wearings. Steaming helps fluff pile that has been crushed.

COMMUNICATING WITH YOUR DRY CLEANER

To assist in the professional removal of stains, take a stained garment promptly to the dry cleaner, and tell them what caused the stain. Areas damaged by attempts at home removal of stains can sometimes be corrected.

CLEANING SEQUINS AND BEADS

If sequins or beads are glued onto a scarf, it should be dry-cleaned. A net should be used in dry-cleaning and the garment should be tested to ensure that beads don't come loose or that bead color doesn't run. If the sequins or beads are sewn onto a washable fabric, it can be handwashed in cool water and Woolite.

DRY-CLEANING METALLICS

It's risky to clean fabrics with metallic thread in them. They should be cleaned with petroleum or fluorocarbons instead of standard dry-cleaning fluid.

REMOVING STAINS BY HAND

Success in stain removal, professionally or at home, is determined by the degree to which dyes and sizings (the finish applied to fabric in manufacture) are colorfast when wet. Do not try to remove a stain yourself if the care label says "Dry Clean Only," if the garment is not colorfast, or if the stain is greasy. Because dyes and sizings tend to discolor with moisture, attempting to remove stains with water is not recommended without first testing the garment for colorfastness. Removal of a concentrated food or beverage stain is difficult. Try to absorb stains before they set by using the tip of a white paper towel to soak up excess liquid. Never scrub or press; it could ruin fabric texture.

STAINS FROM TOILETRIES, PERFUMES, AND ALCOHOL

Perfumes, hairspray, and toiletries contain alcohol, which can cause some dyes on silk to bleed or change color. Allow these products to dry on the body before you dress. Remove stains from alcoholic beverages as soon as possible. Some silk dyes, especially those in blue and green, are sensitive to alkalies, found in facial soaps, shampoos, detergents, and toothpastes. If color loss results from contact with these products, bring the scarf to your dry cleaner to discuss restoration.

GREASY STAINS

Oil and grease stains can be removed with a dry-cleaning fluid. It should be lightly blotted, never rubbed, as "chafing" and texture distortion could result. Spot remover, chlorine bleach, or an enzyme pre-soak may damage delicate fibers. Take it to the dry cleaner promptly.

NON-GREASY STAINS

To remove from a colorfast garment, place the stain facedown on dry paper towels. Sprinkle the back of the stain with a few drops of Woolite diluted in water, then wet the area. Change towels as they soak up the liquid and stain, until the stain is gone.

REMOVING STAINS FROM WOOL

(Follow the recommendations of the Wool Bureau.)

SALAD DRESSING OR LIPSTICK STAINS

Apply spot-cleaning spray or fluid and rinse with soapy water.

COFFEE OR TEA

Dab with mild soapy water or glycerine; rinse with 5% hydrogen peroxide in water or with white vinegar.

INK

Soak in rubbing alcohol, rinse with cool water. Apply hairspray, let it dry, and brush it away.

RED WINE OR COLORED LIQUIDS

Apply absorbent powder or salt, brush away, soak with mineral water or cool water; rinse with rubbing alcohol.

PRESSING

A rolled edge on a scarf should not be pressed. If pressed, it has to be reopened, pressed flat, rerolled, and restitched.

FABRIC REPAIR

Most woven fabrics can be rewoven by dry cleaners or tailors. Unraveled scarves can be rerolled and sewn.

DRY CLEANING BEFORE STORAGE

This is recommended, as fresh stains that are not yet visible or oxydized will become fixed if stored unclean.

STORING WITH PLASTIC

Natural fibers need to breathe. Storing white fabrics in cellophane will cause them to yellow from oxidation. Keep them uncovered, or covered in a cloth.

COLOR FADING

Many brightly colored fabrics fade from exposure to sunlight or artificial light. Some blue and green dyes fade exceptionally fast, especially on silk. Store garments in closets away from light.

MOTH PROTECTION

Mothballs and cedar chips are standard protection from moth infestation of woolens. However, according to Jeeves of Belgravia, the luxury dry cleaner in New York City, the most certain prevention is derived from paraflakes—a mothproofing product sold under different brand names in hardware and housewares stores. Dark woolens can be stored in plastic; white fabrics will risk yellowing in plastic.

DO-IT-YOURSELF

Making other things out of scarves is facilitated by Simplicity Patterns, which offers a pattern kit containing eight different styles of handbag, including a tote, drawstring, and envelope bag. Available through fabric stores nationwide, Simplicity's accessories selection is extensive, and includes patterns for can-opener covers, bedside caddies, toaster-oven and microwave covers, and table skirts. For information, write: Simplicity Pattern Company, 901 Wayne Street, Niles, MI 49121.

PILLOW HOW-TO

Machine-stitch cotton sheeting or canvas to same-size scarves; then machine stitch the edges together (inside out) leaving a small opening on one side. Turn the sewn pillow case right side out through the hole; then stuff with polyester foam. To close the opening, handstitch. As these pillows should be dry-cleaned, not washed, a zipper closure isn't necessary.

TO COVER A FRAME

To cover a frame requires a fabric with texture that will provide some loft, or slip resistance, against wood. The scarf works best when stiched to cotton backing in crosshatched rows before it is attached to a wooden canvas stretcher available at art supply shops. The stretcher is sold in pieces that join together at an angle. The fabric is stapled snugly at the back of each piece and then the pieces are pushed together.

where.

A Chic Simple store looks out on the world beyond its shop window. Items are practical and comfortable and will work with pieces bought elsewhere. The store can be a cottage industry or a global chain, but even with an international vision it is still rooted in tradition, quality, and value.

United States

CALIFORNIA

AMERICAN RAG CIE
150 South La Brea
Los Angeles, CA 90036
213/935-3154

MAXFIELD
8825 Melrose Avenue
Los Angeles, CA 90069
310/274-8800

MIO
2035 Fillmore Street
San Francisco, CA 94115
415/931-5620

OBIKO
794 Sutter Street
San Francisco, CA 94115
415/775-2882

ZOË
2400 Fillmore Street
San Francisco, CA 94115
415/929-0441

FLORIDA

BURDINE'S
1675 Meridian Avenue
Miami Beach, FL 33139
305/835-5151
Catalogue available

GEORGIA

RICH'S
Lenox Square Shopping Mall
3393 Peachtree Road
Atlanta, Georgia 30326
404/231-2611

HAWAII

LIBERTY HOUSE
Ala Moana
Waikiki Beach
Honolulu, HI 96845
808/941-2345

ILLINOIS

ULTIMO
114 East Oak Street
Chicago, IL 60611
312/787-0906

MASSACHUSETTS

FILENE'S
426 Washington Street
Boston, MA 02101
617/357-2100
617/357-2601 for U.S.
listings

LOUIS, BOSTON
234 Berkeley Street
Boston, MA 02116
617/262-6100
800/225-5135 for U.S.
listings

MISSISSIPPI

THE ROGUE
4450 I-55 North
Jackson, MI 39211
601/362-6383

NEW YORK

BERGDORF GOODMAN
754 Fifth Avenue
New York, NY 10019
212/753-7300

CANAL JEANS
504 Broadway
New York, NY 10012
212/226-1130

CASHMERE•CASHMERE
840 Madison Avenue
New York, NY 10021
212/988-5252

GABAY'S OUTLET
(BLOOMINGDALE'S
SECONDS)
225 First Avenue
New York, NY 10003
212/254-3180

GALERIES LAFAYETTE
Trump Tower
10 East 57th Street
New York, NY 10022
212/355-0022

GEOFFREY BEENE
783 Fifth Avenue
New York, NY 10022
212/398-0800

MUSEUM OF MODERN ART DESIGN STORE
44 West 53rd Street
New York, NY 10019
212/767-1050

WHITNEY MUSEUM SHOP
945 Madison Avenue
New York, NY 10021
212/570-3613

ZORAN
214 Sullivan Street
New York, NY 10012
212/674-6087
(by appointment)

PENNSYLVANIA

LAST CALL AT NEIMAN MARCUS
1455 Franklin Mills Circle
Franklin Mills Mall
Philadelphia, PA 19154
215/637-5900

NAN DUSKIN
210 Rittenhaus Square
Philadelphia, PA 19103
215/735-6400

AGNÈS B.
116 Prince Street
New York, NY 10012
212/925-4649

ANN TAYLOR
3 East 57th Street
New York, NY 10022
212/832-2010

BANANA REPUBLIC
130 East 59th Street
New York, NY 10022
212/751-5570
212/446-3995 for U.S.
listings

BARNEYS NEW YORK
111 Seventh Avenue
New York, NY 10011
212/929-9000
800/777-0087 for U.S.
listings

HENRI BENDEL
712 Fifth Avenue
New York, NY 10019
212/247-1100

BENETTON
Galleria Passarella 2
2/79-47-49 for stores in Italy
and worldwide

BLOOMINGDALE'S
1000 Third Avenue
New York, NY 10022
212/355-5900 for U.S.
listings

BROOKS BROTHERS
346 Madison Avenue
New York, NY 10017
212/682-8800
800/444-1613 for catalogue
and store listings

BURBERRYS LTD.
9 East 57th Street
New York, NY 10022
212/371-5010
800/284-8480 for U.S.
listings

CALVIN KLEIN
199 Boylston Street
Boston, MA 02167
617/527-8975
800/223-6808 for U.S.
listings

CELINE
51 East 57th Street
New York, NY 10022
212/486-9700

CHANEL BOUTIQUE
5 East 57th Street
New York, NY 10022
212/355-5050

DAYTON'S
700 On The Mall
Minneapolis, MN 55402
612/375-2200

DILLARD'S PARK
PLAZA
Markham and University
Little Rock, AR 72205
501/661-0053

EMILIO PUCCI
Palazzo Pucci
Via dei Pucci 6r
Florence, Italy
55/28-30-61

EMPORIO ARMANI
110 Fifth Avenue
New York, NY 10011
212/727-3240
212/570-1122 for
international listings

THE GAP
1 Harrison Street
San Francisco, CA 94105
415/777-0250

GIORGIO ARMANI
815 Madison Avenue
New York, NY 10021
212/988-9191
212/570-1122 for
international listings

GUCCI
685 Fifth Avenue
New York, NY 10022
212/826-2600
201/867-8800 for
international listings

HERMÈS
11 East 57th Street
New York, NY 10022
212/751-3181
212/759-7585 for U.S.
listings

ISSEY MIYAKE
992 Madison Avenue
New York, NY 10021
212/439-7822

5-3-10 Minami Aoyama
Minato-ku, Tokyo
3/3499-6476

J. CREW
203 Front Street
New York, NY 10038
800/782-8244 for U.S.
listings; catalogue available

THE JOSEPH ABBOUD
STORE
37 Newbury Street
Boston, MA 02116
617/266-4200

THE LIMITED
2 Limited Parkway
Columbus, OH 43230
614/479-2000 for U.S.
listings

LORD & TAYLOR
424 Fifth Avenue
New York, NY 10018
212/391-3344

R.H. MACY & CO., INC.
(Bullock's, I. Magnin,
Aeropostale)
Macy's Herald Square
151 West 34th Street
New York, NY 10001
212/695-4400 for East Coast
listings
415/393-3457 for West Coast
listings

MAY D & F
(Foley's, Robinson's, May)
16th at Tremont Place
Denver, CO 80202
303/620-9005 for U.S.
listings

METROPOLITAN
MUSEUM OF ART
MUSEUM SHOPS
Fifth Avenue and 82nd Street
New York, NY 10028
212/535-7710 for U.S.
listings

NEIMAN MARCUS
1618 Main Street
Dallas, TX 75201
214/741-6911

N. PEAL
37 Burlington Arcade
London W1V 9AE
71/493-9220
800/446-9678 for U.S.
listings

NORDSTROM
1501 Fifth Avenue
Seattle, WA 98101
206/628-2111
800/695-8000 for U.S.
listings; catalogue available

PARISIAN
2100 River Chase Galleria
Birmingham, AL 35244
205/987-4200
205/940-4000 for U.S.
listings

PENDLETON SHOPS
489 Fifth Avenue
New York, NY 10022
212/661-0655

POLO/RALPH LAUREN
867 Madison Avenue
New York, NY 10021
212/606-2100
212/318-7000 for U.S.
listings

SAK'S FIFTH AVENUE
611 Fifth Avenue
New York, NY 10022
212/753-4000 for U.S.
listings

SALVATORE
FERRAGAMO
LADIES APPAREL,
SHOES AND
ACCESSORIES
717 Fifth Avenue
New York , NY 10022
212/759-3822
212/838-9470 for U.S.
listings

TALBOTS
175 Beal Street
Hingham, MA 02043
800/8 TALBOT for
international listings
800/992-9010 for catalogue

TIFFANY & CO.
Fifth Avenue and 57th
Street
New York, NY 10022
212/755-8000
212/605-4612 for
international listings

URBAN OUTFITTERS
1801 Walnut Street
Philadelphia, PA 19103
215/569-3131
215/564-2313 for U.S.
listings

YSL
38 rue du Faubourg Saint-
Honoré
75008 Paris, France

ZONA
97 Greene Street
New York, NY 10012
212/925-6750

SERVICE

UNCLE SAM UMBRELLA
SHOP
161 West 57th Street
New York, NY 10019
212/247-7163
*(makes 4-rib umbrellas from
scarves)*

UNITS
2485 Merritt Drive
Garland, TX 75041
214/271-5533
*(stores around the country
have stylists on the premises)*

CATALOGUES AND
MAIL ORDER

NATIONAL WILDLIFE
NATURE GIFTS
National Wildlife
Federation
1400 Sixteenth Street, N.W.
Washington, DC 20036
800/432-6564

WATHNE
1095 Cranbury South River
Road, Suite 8
Jamesburg, NJ 08831
609/655-8222

INTERNATIONAL
LISTINGS

Australia

MELBOURNE

GEORGES
162 Collins Street 2000
3/283-5535

SYDNEY

DAVID JONES
86-108 Cartheray Street
2000
2/266-5544

GRACE BROS.
436 George Street 2000
2/218-1111

THE KEN DONE
GALLERY
21 Nurses Walk
The Rocks
2/ 247-2740

Canada

MONTREAL

CRÉATION ELLES-
TOILES
3971 St. Denis
514/845-5674

LA CACHE
1353 Greene
514/935-4361 for national
listings

TORONTO

ALFRED SUNG
Hazelton Lanes
87 Avenue Road
M5R 3L2
416/922-9226

CREEDS
45 Bloor Street West
416/923-1000

FRIDA CRAFT STORE
39 Front Street East
M5E 1B3
416/366-3169

HOLT RENFREW
50 Bloor Street West
416/922-2333 for national
listings; Point of View
catalogue available

IRA BERG
1510 Yonge Street
416/922-9100

VANCOUVER

BACCI'S
2788 Granville Street
604/733-4933

France

PARIS

AGNÈS B.
6, rue du Jour
75001
45/08-56-56

AMERICAN RAG
COMPONENTS
9, rue de Turbigo
45/08-96-10

DOROTHÉE BIS STOCK
74, rue d'Alesia
75014
45/42-22-00-45

MANUEL CANOVAS
5, Place Furstemberg
75006
43/26-89-31

GALERIES LAFAYETTE
40, Boulevard Haussmann
75009
42/82-34-56

HERMÈS
24, rue du Faubourg Saint-
Honoré
75008
40/17-47-17

INÈS DE LA
FRESSANGE
14, avenue Montaigne
75008
47/23-64-87

AU PRINTEMPS
64, boulevard Haussmann
75009
42/82-50-00

Germany

BERLIN

SELBACH
Kurfurstendamm 195/196
30/883-2526

HAMBURG

JIL SANDER
Milchstrasse 13
2000
40/553-02173

KAISERSLAUTERN

OTTO KERN
Augustastrasse 1
6/31-84-00-20

MUNICH

MEY & EDLICH
Theatinerstrasse 7
89/290-0590
30/7915030 in Berlin

THERESA
Theatinerstrasse 31
89/224-845

Great Britain

LONDON

TIE RACK, HEAD
OFFICE
Capital Interchange Way
Brentford, Middlesex
TW8 0EX
81/995-1344

BURBERRYS LTD.
165 Regent Street
W1
71/734-4060

EMMETT SHIRTS
300 King's Road
SW3
71/351-7529

GUCCI LTD.
32-33 Old Bond Street
W1
71/235-6707

HARRODS
87-135 Brompton Road
SW1
71/730-1234

HARVEY NICHOLS
109-125 Knightsbridge
SW1
71/235-5000

HERMÈS
155 New Bond Street
W1Y 9PA
71/499-8856

LIBERTY PLC.
210-220 Regent Street
W1R
71/734-1234

MARKS & SPENCER
PLC.
99 Kensington High Street
W8
71/938-3711

MUJI
26 Great Marlborough
Street
W1V HIB
71/494-1197

NEXT PLC
160 Regent Street
W1R 5TA
71/434-2515

TIMNEY & FOWLER
388 King's Road
SW3
71/352-2263

HONG KONG

COURRÈGES
BOUTIQUE
G15 Gloucester Tower
The Landmark
11 Pedder Steet
5/523-3776

CROCODILE
GARMENTS LTD
G/F
50 Connaught Road
5/541-5499 for stores in
Hong Kong, Kowloon, and
New Territories

FOUR SEASONS
GARMENTS
10/F South China
Building, Room B
1-3 Wyndham Street
5/525-9311 for stores in
Hong Kong and Kowloon

Italy

COMO

CENTRO DELLA SETA
via Volta, 64
31/27-98-61
via Bellinzona, 3
31/55-67-93

RATTI
via Cernobbi, 17
31/23-32-62

MILAN

ETRO
via Montenapoleone, 5
2/550201

ZORAN
corso Matteoti, 1A
2/76-00-79-58

ROME

BISES
via Del Gesù, 93
6/67-80-941
6/67-89-156

IL DISCOUNT
DELL'ALTA MODA
via Gesù e Maria, 16/a
no phone

ROMANI
via del Babuino, 94
6/67-92-323

Japan

TOKYO

ISETAN
14-1, Shinjuku, 3-chome
Shinjuku-ku 160
3/3352-1111

MATSUYA GINZA
6-1, Ginza 3-chome
Chou-ku 160
3/3567-1211

MITSUKOSHI
6-16, Ginza 4-chome
Chou-ku 104
3/3241-3311

MITSUMINE
Alpha Grace
2-15-22 Jiyugaoka
Meguro-ku
3/3724-1665

MUJI
4-22-8 Paishidou
Setadayahu
3/3410-2323

PARCO I, II, III
15-1, Udagawa-cho
Shibuya-ku
Tokyo 150
3/3477-5731

SUZUYA
Tamagawa Takashimaya 1F
3-17-1 Tamagawa
Setagaya-ku
3/3709-3394

TAKASHIMAYA
4-4-1 Nihombashi
Chuo-ku 103
3/3211-4111

RESOURCES

COVER FRONT

SILK SCARF - Yves Saint Laurent

BACK

(Clockwise from top left)
COTTON SQUARE - Timney & Fowler;
WATCHBAND - Gene Meyer; SILK
SQUARE - Louis Vuitton; SILK
LEOPARD SQUARE- Yves Saint Laurent

THE SCARF

10 FLORAL CHIFFON SCARF - Chanel
14–15 (From left) SILK POCKET SQUARE -
Gene Meyer; SILK SQUARE - Paloma
Picasso; CHIFFON OBLONG - Echo;
SILK SQUARE - Yves Saint Laurent
16 (From top) CHIFFON SCARF - Gene
Meyer; VELVET OBLONG - Commes
Des Garçons
18 SILK & CASHMERE REVERSIBLE
MUFFLER - Salvatore Ferragamo

20 (Clockwise from top left) SILK SQUARE -
Hermès; SILK SCARVES - Gene Meyer;
PLAID CASHMERE MUFFLER - Isaac
Mizrahi; VELVET PAISLEY SHAWL -
WovenWind
22–23 SILK LEOPARD SQUARE - Yves Saint
Laurent; SILK FLORAL SQUARE - Chanel
24 (From top) SILK & WOOL WRAP
WITH TASSEL - Anichini; SILK POCKET
SQUARE - Gene Meyer; PURPLE RAW
SILK SCARF - Gene Meyer; PINK SILK
SCARF - Gene Meyer; PAISLEY SILK
MUFFLER - Stylist's personal collection;
CASHMERE SCARF - Cashmere • Cashmere;
26 COTTON SQUARE - Timney & Fowler
27 COTTON SQUARE - Souvenir scarf, Paris
28 COTTON BANDANNA - Canal Jeans
30 SILK FLORAL SQUARE - Chanel
33 (From top) CASHMERE MUFFLER -
Cashmere • Cashmere; PLAID WOOL
SHAWL - Isaac Mizrahi; SILK & GOLD
HAND-WOVEN WRAP - WovenWind;
COTTON PAREO - China Seas

WEARING

34 SILK HALTER TOP - Salvatore
Ferragamo; SILK PAISLEY BELT - Etro;
COTTON WRAP - WovenWind; SKIRT -
assorted scarves
36 SILK SQUARE - Yves Saint Laurent
38–39 (From left) POLYESTER OBLONG -
Echo; PLEATED SILK TWILL SQUARE -
Hermès; SILK OBLONG - Gene Meyer
40 CHIFFON FLORAL SQUARE - Yves
Saint Laurent

42 **SHEER WOVEN METALLIC RIBBON MUFFLER** - DebraMoises

43 **SILK SQUARE** - Hermès; **WOOL MUFFLER** - Joseph Abboud

44 (From left) **CASHMERE MUFFLER** - Cashmere · Cashmere; **WOOL CHALLIS SQUARE** - Paloma Picasso

46 **PUCKERED RAYON SQUARE** - bought in Chinese market, New York

48 (From left) **WOOL CHALLIS OBLONG WITH SILKSCREENED STRIPS** - Bottega Veneta; **TWO COTTON SCARVES** - private collection

50 **SILK OBLONG HALTER TOP** - Paloma Picasso; **SILK BRA TOP** - Gucci

51 **SILK SQUARES** - Emilio Pucci

52 **SILK SARONG SKIRT** - Timney & Fowler; **WOOL SARONG DRESS** - Timney & Fowler

55 **CASHMERE BLANKET** - Anichini; **BELT** - The Gap

54 **SILK SEERSUCKER WRAP SKIRT** - Marisa Toriggino; **COTTON BATIK HALTER DRESS AND WAIST BELT** - China Seas

56 **ANTIQUE FABRIC DHOTI** - Stylist's personal collection

58 **SILK OBLONG WRAP** - Geoffrey Beene

60-61 **REVERSIBLE SILK BROCADE WRAP** - DebraMoises

62 **TULLE WRAP** - Geoffrey Beene

ACCESSORIES

64 **PILLOWS** - Gene Meyer

66 **HANDBAG & SCARF** - Emilio Pucci

68 (Clockwise from top left) **WATCHBAND** - Gene Meyer; **SHOES** - Charles Jourdan; **EYEGLASS CASE** - Emilio Pucci; **UMBRELLA** - Salvatore Ferragamo

72 **SCARVES FOR LAMPSHADES** (from top) - Gene Meyer; Echo scarves; Commes Des Garçons

74 **SILK SQUARE** - Louis Vuitton

76 **FRAMED SILK SCARF** - Juraku Scarf

78 **REVERSIBLE RAYON SCARF** - Felissimo **MANNEQUINS ON WHEELS** - Courtesy of Geoffrey Beene **MANNEQUINS WITH LEGS** - Courtesy of Adel Rootstein

QUOTES

Quotations not acquired directly through an interview were drawn from the following sources:

2 **ROBERT HERRICK,** *The Oxford Dictionary of Quotations* (1955 Edition).

11 **DONNA KARAN,** *Vogue* (April 1993).

12–13 **ISADORA DUNCAN,** *After Egypt: Isadora Duncan & Mary Cassatt* (New York: Dutton, 1990).

21 **OSCAR WILDE,** *The Artist as Critic.*

26 **GIANNI VERSACE,** *Vogue* (April 1993).

96 **JAMES FENIMORE COOPER,** *The American Democrat* (1838).

ACKNOWLEDGMENTS

The Association of Professional Drycleaners & Launderers, Geoffrey Beene, Rosie Boycott, The Camel Hair & Cashmere Institute of America, Beth Chang, Tony Chirico, M. Scott Cookson, Lauri Del Commune, Dina Dell'Arciprete, Chris Di Maggio, Diandra Douglas, Michael Drazen, Jane Friedman, The Gilbert Center of Uncle Sam's Umbrellas, Janice Goldklang, Joanne Harrison, Patrick Higgins, Katherine Hourigan, Andy Hughes, The International Fabric Care Institute, Carol Janeway, Jeeves of Belgravia, Oshima Kazuko, Nicholas Latimer, Karen Leh, David Leith, Mali Lipener, William Loverd, Martha Malovany, Anne McCormick, James McFate of the Wool Bureau, Sonny Mehta, Gene Meyer, Motoe of Woven Wind, Misako Noda, Helen O'Hagen, Paloma Picasso, Lynn Roberts, Adel Rootstein, Hellyn Sher, C. P. Smith, Anne-Lise Spitzer, Meg Stebbins, Robin Swados, Patricia Tisi, Kim Turner, Mish Tworkowski, Kenneth Valenti, Diane Von Furstenberg, Shelley Wanger, Wayne Wolf, Alice Wong, Laura Zigman

A NOTE ON THE TYPE

The text of this book was set in New Baskerville, the ITC version of the typeface called Baskerville, which itself is a facsimile reproduction of types cast from molds made by John Baskerville (1706–1775) from his designs. Baskerville's original typeface was one of the forerunners of the type style known to printers as the "modern face"—a "modern" of the period A.D. 1800.

SEPARATION AND FILM PREPARATION BY
APPLIED GRAPHICS TECHNOLOGIES
Carlstadt, New Jersey

PRINTED AND BOUND BY
**IMPRESORA DONNECO INTERNACIONAL,
S.A. De C.V.
Reynosa, Mexico**

"A refined simplicity is the characteristic of all high-bred deportment in every country."

JAMES FENIMORE COOPER,

The American Democrat